THE RIBS OF DEATH

THE RIBS OF DEATH

Paul Zimmer

OCTOBER HOUSE INC · NEW YORK

Published by October House Inc.
55 West 13th Street, New York

Copyright © 1967 by Paul Zimmer
All rights reserved

Certain of these poems have appeared in the following publica-
tions: Virginia Quarterly Review, Prairie Schooner, The
Northwest Review, The Southern Poetry Review, Poet and
Critic, The Galley Sail Review, and Yankee. "First Mate
Joseph Conrad" appeared in *Poetry: An Introduction and
Anthology* by Charles S. Felver and Martin Nurmi © 1967
by Charles E. Merrill Books, Inc.

Library of Congress catalog card number 67-18851
Printed by Clarke & Way, Inc., New York, U.S.A.
First Edition

TO SUE, WITH LOVE

"I was all ear,
And took in strains that might create a soul
Under the ribs of death . . ."
John Milton, *Comus* 559–561

Contents

I

PHINEAS, FLUTING, WANDA, AND ALPHONSE

Phineas Within and Without

Phineas dwelled midst lives of many pieces,
In bird flocks and fish schools.

Phineas fell when the grey birds rose,
He drank when the fish were breathing;
He lived so long midst the many pieces
He began to learn their whole.

He puzzled at the small lives,
The twist of a beak or fin;
And marveled at the large lives,
The flick of a school or flock.

Phineas fell when the grey birds rose,
He drank when the fish were breathing;
He lived so long within their without,
He died amidst their whole.

Phineas and Organ as God and Landscape

My slightest touch upon the great gates
Of this golden city creates a siege.
Before the lucent forest that surrounds it,
My fists upon the echoes sound like bees
At buttercups. I strain all seasons
Through the bellows, all weather rich or poor.
I stagger lightning down the flues, swell rain,
And draw the sunshine with my green lobation.
I blow the breezes choirwise in the wind chests,
And flap the shutters like great solo birds.
I forgive all sins that drop like full notes
On the hills and streams. I permit its evil,
And run its good high through the cloudy flutes.

Phineas in Heat

Nude in the dew,
"Sweet-sweet, chew-chew,"
The Buntings whisper
In Phinny's ear.
Hard grows his groin,
With a pain in his loin,
And the grass has lips,
And breasts, and hips.

Phineas in Light and Dark

I

The bees do not sting our Phineas,
But fill his ears with flowery juices.
The wolves do not race to bite him,
But pas de deux around his feet.
The fox is a squirrel to Phineas,
And the snake is a garland of larkspur.

II

The teeth of lightning gnaw
Upon his cheeks, as thunder
Rubs his eardrums raw,
And spits across his nerves.
Raindrops crawl upon his neck
Like blowflies fresh from
A rotting corpse. The stone
Is cold and jagged to his hams.
The thrashing trees are full
Of irritations, and the flowers,
Dripping stupidly, enrage him.

The Poet Bequeaths his Frustrations to Phineas

It comforts me to think all storms
Compound to frazzle Phineas,
All mud suspends to sog him,
All wind expands to knock him.

Let the birds make flux upon
His head, place all cow cakes
In his path, and leprous skunks
Beneath his perceptive nostrils.

Give him my heat and my cold,
My fear and my temper.
Let his white palms sweat,
And his voice rise and fall
With the temperature.

Lord Fluting Dreams of America on the Eve of his Departure from Liverpool

Purple Indians pas de bourrée
Around a Chippendale totem pole.
The Ute dips to the Crow,
And curtsies to the Navajo,
While the forest in its wig and stole
Claps its leaves politely.

Cotton and tobacco plants cluster
On the backland hills like
Plaster on a Spanish cloister.
The rivers and the lakes
Are filled with plumèd bass
Who browse urbanely on the watercress.

The sylvan trail to Oregon
Is thronged with gentle post chaise
Gliding toward great fortune;
For this is where the buffalo turn
Broadside to the hunting horns,
And gold is strained like sunshine
Through the heath.

Lord Fluting in America

Some ass has slapped mud
In the chinks of my house,
But the wind grinds through
To fray my ripening nostrils.
I find that misery is a complex thing,
A subtle blend of bound bowels,
Damp feet, and unwashed clothing.

I have become so fluttery and cold.
Where are the wigwams full of gold?

When the frost is eased out of
The sod the sun becomes as cheeky
As a fractured hornet's nest,
And my food is curdled like
   Once-eaten gruel upon the tins.

Oh, I have become so fluttery and old.
Where are the teepees filled with gold?

I am too temperate for these extremes,
But I am so full of heat and cold
I know if I returned that time
Would end me short of home.

I, Fluting, am so fluttery with cold,
And I have never seen the wigwams full of gold.

Wanda and the Unwashed Wise Man

It certainly wasn't his seeping beak
That won me, those raggedy ears,
That rancid beard, or
His body full of corners.
It was that beautiful mumbling.
His tongue made up for a score of warts,
And his mind for all his ill wind.

One day he stopped me on the street
And said, "The hydroxyl anamnesis of numen
Is related to the technocratic microtone,"
And I was finished! Speared and spitted!
"The eschatology of atropine is null,
As vorticism is to fanxensyndrome."
God!

Give me words to sinews,
Syllables to oily muscles!
The tenacity of that quick tongue
Was stronger than those unsponged armpits,
And to me his very sounds were aphrodisiac.

Wanda, in Love with Phineas

Last night the wind was fingers and kisses,
Pine trees were sighs, cobwebs semen,
And rain the earnest sweat of lovers.
Last night I was loved with finitude.
Hereafter all will measure to this.
Last night the warm birds moaned
On the branches, the dark came down,
The light fell up, and stars
Perceptively coiled about the moon.

Wanda Petrified

The jellyfish swim vaguely
Over the stony body of Wanda.
The delicate crystals of her face
Are craggy through the lenses
Of their bodies. Her arms cemented
In their sockets will never raise her
From the sea again to kiss her lover.
She has changed from flesh
To quartz, with gypsum eyes
And teeth of calcite. Cell by cell
And inch by inch her tenderness
Has hardened, till now she lies
The coldest rock beneath the sea.

Alphonse Loses his Love in Autumn

Slant to the smoky wind, Alphonse.
Watch the spiders spitting
In the curl of fallen leaves,
And color ground to a pulpy opaque.
Is sadness a season? So it would seem.
The death of puny flowers is unhappily complete;
Next year's blossoms cannot replace these
That grind so pitifully upon the wind.
The promise of snow is a six-sided melancholy.
Love is chapped and ragged, tucked with
Too ripe apples in the mulch,
Waiting to freeze brittle under winter.

Ambushed and Beaten, Alphonse Crawls Back to his Unloved Life

Move. Keep something moving.
Scrawl your crawl with fingertips,
Lest your flesh begin to melt
Into the rocks that grind it.
Curse the walleyed ants
That watch your tedious passage,
Curse the sun that peels your neck,
And curse the moon for
A sterile, indifferent apple.
The only thing that day and night
Provide is your direction.
The only thing you salvage are
Your bones and your invectives;
But scribble sand and bruise the moss.
Return to your potential.
Being unloved is better than
Being loveless.

Alphonse is Invisible to Wanda

Oh Wanda, your sight is osmotic
Through my body. Your words
Are for some bones or flesh
Behind mine, and your smile
Is for some smile beyond my lips.

Yet, I would tamp your myopic words
Deep into my eardrums, and bring
Your face to my lips, but I
Forever am within, and never
At the point of your dear focus.

Aged Alphonse Disparages Himself

How despicable I am! How unloved!
How sour of armpit, askew of nose,
And piddling of penis; how filmy brained.
Not mother, dog, nor lady has ever
Loved me that I know of.

How loathsome!
How full of unloveable smells, wrinkles,
Warts, greases, scabs, knots, sores, scars,
And hideous twists of bone and flesh.

I cannot even love myself.
When I die I'll disappear unloved like steam,
Like shade, like time, for all time.

Alphonse Imagines what the People's Thoughts
will be when he is Gone

Where is that gaseous Alphonse
Whose round head used to rise
Upon a string above ours,
Whose bat wing eyebrows
Lofted him above our heads?
Where is he, whose words
Between his custardy teeth,
Dropped to us like stale bread
To the geese? Ah sadness!
He is gone like ancient light waves,
Like fingerprints on icicles.
Invisible and unloved he slipped
Through our blockish fingers.
Ah sin, our obtundity, our sin!
Now we would give him all
Our love, if only he returned.

II

IN THUNDER, LIGHTNING, OR IN RAIN

The Covens of North Berwick

"For a combined effort the witches of North Berwick . . . met together to aid their master in de-
stroying James VI of Scotland."

The God of the Witches, Margaret Murray

As Gilly Duncan played a reel
Upon the devil's Jew's Harp,
Men turned nine times widdershins
And six times did the crones.

With a hissing sprinkled cat
And limbs of a Berwick corpse
Richard Graham stirred the sea
And howled for the regal ship.

Barbara Napier broke her chants
And saw the king's nose
Fold across his cheek
Above the rancid fire.

Agnes Sampson strung a toad
And watched the dripping venom
Gather in an oyster shell,
Black for the royal collar.

Despite the devil's treason
King James stood whole in Scotland,
And witches groaned in thraws,
And told their sins in ashes.

Two Studies of Mary Dodd

I *The Man*

Yes sir, I remember Mary Dodd,
As wicked as a jay bird, and enough
To prickle hair out of your chest.
She was cut out of the cheesy stuff

That sets a hound to straining
At the moon, and once a week
At dawn, when dark slid down
The hills to gather in the creek,

She muttered into town for food,
Colder than the bottom of a stone.
She shuffled in her boots when there
Was not a drop to chill her bones,

And someone claimed the puddles foamed
Before she stirred them with her skirts.
Her son and husband, gone for years,
Had wrinkled with the town dirt,

And left her with a string of grief
To strum her lonely mind upon.
So struck, she tasseled every fence
Post with a can to scoop the sun.

Dead now for thirty years, her cabin
Swallowed by a swell of green,
I recall the day she died, battered
To her dirty knees by men so lean

They thought they could smell money
In the must that netted up her wall.
And now she's gone these years, except
For some like me who can recall

How cold her body was to fingers of
A boy who had gone out an afternoon
To taunt old Mary Dodd to death,
And found her lying dead too soon.

II *The Boy*

Oh Jesus, Mary Dodd is murdered,
Her skull as red as any matted rose!
I found her lying like a pile of clay
Beneath the "Stay Out" signs she'd chalked
Upon her walls. Someone has thumped
The blood out of her veins!
                                I crept up
To pelt her cabin with new apples,
And there she was, her eyelids horny
As old turtle shells, and cheeks as green
As apples I had dropped. The blood
Had run its petals down her head.
And her teeth were dead as yellow leaves.

As I turned to run the sun was smearing
On the cans she'd tacked to fence posts,
And in the woods some wormless bird
Was shrieking with its hunger.
                                Oh Jesus,
I have been so scared at night I thought
The moon was raining bats, but Mary Dodd,
So green in sun, has made the daylight
Dark with fear.

Seven Musicians, Buttoned in Red

Like branches parrying in woods,
Like clutched buds
With the wind across them,
The seven musicians, buttoned in red,
Play at the heels of witchery,
Their side drums daddy-mammying,
And krummhorns wheezing,
With cornet and sackbutts baying.

Evil wavers at their approach.
All maledictions,
Curses, spells are flushed out
Of the oak nodes and blown into
The snare head sky. Lord,
How they play con brio! Loud
Enough to crack
The devil's tympanum with resonance.

Witches claw the bark of trees
In mortal fear
Of their septettos. This year
No cats will be beheaded, nor
Horntoads wrung for venom.
The seven musicians, buttoned in red,
Play the tunes
That clear the woods of witchery.

The Return of the Griffin

No buckshot could clear it from our skies,
No reason reconfine it to its yellow pages.
The shadows of its wings, as terrible
As thunderheads, beat about our horses
And our children. And all that spring,
As trees forgot their birds, we found
Its work like mangled roses in the grass.
Through the summer and the fall we heard
Its fluting and many felt its beak impale
Their hearts, and in winter the blood drops
Burned within the snow like peepholes
Into hell. And no one—no one could say
What energy had brought the griffin back
Into our lands to force our penance,
Rip our horses, and eat our steaming hearts.

The Coming of the Fairies to New England

She heard the stitching of the earth worms
As they worked the floor that night,
And the moon was like a carp eye,
Hungry at the doorway. No breeze,
And yet the pine cones rang like bells
Within the trees. Brian ten days gone,
And now she knew that something
Was afoot. That day, as she had bent
To check the well, two faces wrinkled
In the water, and one was not her own.
They have jumped the sea, she thought,
Splitting wave tips with their toes
From Ireland to the coast of Maine.
They have come, the whistle-voiced
And hairless, and those with carcasses
Like bears, to set me dreaming of
The dancing land beyond the nearest hills.

For three nights the fairies called to her,
The old tongue trilling through new hills,
And then she heard no more of them.
Barred owls laughed now in the woods,
And toads blew echoes from the well.
The moon turned back to molded cheese,
And pine cones lost their clappers.
When Brian came they listened to the breeze
For traces of their ever-dancing feet,
But never heard of them again.
Perhaps they had been killed by Iroquois,
Turned to smoke beneath the chanting
Of the masked man. Perhaps the small pox
Chewed their filmy bodies down to nothing,
Or the great new land, too full of sun
For ancient shadows, swallowed them into itself.

The Witch of Benjamin County

When she lay clawing the weekday puddles
Of the street, a rammed fish broken wide
Under the hate of trees, whipping foam
With fingertips that hinged like brass,

Emma cursed this green county for a dogyard
Of scent and said, if she wished,
It would be snuffed out like sunset shaved
By the Benjamin Hills. And we wondered

As she raged higher than a crowd,
As we had wondered at the sundered cattle,
And dogs that vomited green mist,
And our children off to hound the parish

In a corner of fingers. We had blown
On the green sticks for years to make them
Dry, and she was to straddle them
This day, filling the belly of some flame.

Running grey, we raised her
To the mound, but Emma splashed
Her terror out, scraping
Her own match on the sky.

The Horned Man

It was a shiver like to ice my skull
That made me look to brown stag's steaming head.
The thought like cold rain pricked into my neck,
The inside of the stag runs warm and red.

I cannot say if devils said it to me.
The thought rang clear like icicles when strummed.
I pierced brown stag for heat within his head,
And his heartbeat shrank and his nostrils fumed.

The head was struck before I thought it off;
And I strung it from an oak to feed the wind.
That night, while bogies hissed, I tiptoed from the town,
And only Robin Good knows how I sinned.

I pulled the antlered head about my ears
And felt the dark blood crawl upon my nose.
Through brown stag's eyes I saw the bowstrings drawn,
And mad as Joan I danced to miss the arrows.

That was when my townsmen found me there
And dragged me to you as the devil's spy.
And I will cook because I cannot prove
My body and my mind have sinned, not I.

King Criswell in his Draughty Castle

In spring this mossy castle
Runs so warm about me. The new vines claw
The sweating walls more lustily
Than vikings, and great owls
Will lay their eggs

On eagles' nests in niches.
Water in the green moat curdles with mosquitoes,
And in the windows spiders ride
A slack of web into a breeze.
But there are only

Stains of wine upon the floor
To bring my armies to my mind. In corners
Are the blackened chains that used
To hold my wolves to circles,
And one can sniff

The reechy blood that flakes
Off from the collars. I clap my filthy hands
To no one now. An army full of
Thumping, booming hearts, and
Their anaemic king

Outlasts them all! But ah!
Before the echoes came this castle rang with
Manliness, and knights were made
To prove they had some teeth
Behind their beards.

Barococo Dreams

I Baroque Dream

There are more than peacocks in Poitiers tonight,
More than slight partita and treble shawm vibrato.
There is nothing light about the clamp of night
Upon this yard, the moon a curl of gut not fit
To bow upon. Here lovers shed their gentil sweat
Away from where the ladies twirl like froth
Within their escorts' arms. No rain could arbitrate
Between the rapiers arcing like bright fans
Inside the shadows of a dark, insidious hate.
The walls of palaces are fraught with hideous beasts
And imps applauding the performance of the court.

II Rococo Dream

Even the priest's face in the candlelight is carved.
"Oh cherub-lily-cherub-lily-cherub-lily-cherub,"
Chirp the feathered angels in the half-lit nave.

And pallid, painted Christ is risen in the arches
Held by Samson, Simon, Issachar and Saul,
Whose muscles tense like clusters of seashells.

Within this panoply of plaster, in its grooves
And niches cut like myriad stoney ears,
Roll centuries of soft confiteors
High in vaults where only saints can hear.

The Cross-Eyed Knight is Scattered and Regathered

I

The tapestries of the cross-eyed knight
Are moth dung now. His biceps
Are stitched and pierced with worms.
The stars and fleur-de-lis of his shield
Are flakes of lead in a manor garden.
The gold crown of his liege is somewhere
In a looted vase. The knight rusts.
Like a battered jousting horn
He is beyond a burst of air.

II

The sun smears across trumpet blasts,
And the knight's lungs strain with air.
The pure gold of his king's crown
Flashes the enamel of his heraldry.
Within the muscles of the cross-eyed knight
The worms unstitch and unpierce.
Unrusted and demothed the lubricated
Cross eyed-knight rides to victory again
Across the tapestries of thread and turf.

The Death of Peace

I *The King Prepares, and the Plot*

On the square
The birds grew tight within their feathers,
And the galleys blew like geese upon the bay.
The cannons in the hills scooped practice crators,
And we heard the swordsman bellow at his dummy.

In the palace
Queen Juanita sawed her courtly fingernails
As young King Cruz laid out his ancient chessboard
And dusted off the pawns. Outside the walls
The king's own bard sang epics in the courtyard.

At the noon
My friend, Mantilla, the village drunkard's son,
And I, because of wars, the fatherless,
Decided on our plan to steal the queen
And hold her as a trigger for the peace.

II *A Note to Mantilla*

Come soon.
The wretched girl is wormy with her fright.
Though her teeth are like cold lemon rinds,
And her eyes are droplets in a spider's web,
She is sure I will attempt her.
Devils blush before I touch her!
A fitting wife for a warring king she is!
        Come soon, Mantilla.
I would rather die in war
Than hold a hag as ransom for the peace.
What king would snuff his guns

To succor such a queen?
      Come, Mantilla.
Peace is not so sweet.
Back to back we'll fight the war,
And leave the world to the shrews.

III   *The War Clerk's Entry*

On this day we planted all our dead seed
In a greenless field, and let the vultures
Make their droppings for the markers.

Into one deep hole we rolled their skulls,
Six-thousand string, like withered apples,
And left the earth to swallow up their peace.

III

THE DIFFICULT MIRROR

Ohio Summer Night

The hour was stitched by the abdomens
Of lightning bugs . . . twelve midnight,
The time of train hoots and cat fights
In Ohio August. Through the screens

The smell of Morning-glories sprayed
In little squares until I fell asleep.
Lord, of what did I dream so deeply
In those uncomplicated days?

I had no images or metres to devise,
No manly trade to ply except the art
Of shagging flies or catching carp,
And lying sun-wise in the crab grass.

Perhaps I grew my symbols in the night
And tucked them deep for future use.
Perhaps the rhythm of my dreaming
Rolled in stanzas till the light.

The Tunnel-Visioned Man Striding
Through the Jungle

Though I hear the shrieks
Of hordes of birds,
One bird at a time
Mars my small sky;
Midst all the roaring
And the rending,
But one lion leaps
Upon the zebra;
And despite his thunder,
The elephant is
But an eye,
A trunk, or tusk.
This landscape is either green
Or brown or blue,
Never a combination.
It is puzzling.
I hear snake
Locking with snake,
Boar charging boar,
Tiger eating tiger,
But I cannot see them.
There are no combinations.
There are no groups,
No tangle and dimension,
But one lion,
One boar,
One snake,
One bird,
One tiger,
One vision.
Mine.

On a Statue of the Virgin in my Grade School

Mornings the Virgin wore her halo like a pie pan.
Later when the sun was turning in the plaster rays
She shone enough to crush the serpent underfoot
With her nine toes (as one was bitten white as salt).

Her garment was of blue in folds, unspoiled blue.
Deep within the blue was blue, and so without;
Not blurred by chalk dust, chipped or bleached
By nothing; blue as blue beside it, nothing bluer.

So stark that she seemed thrown, she stood
Upon the curve of earth with love but not
The slightest quivering to show she was a mother,
And for boys had stood like this for centuries.

Afternoons she gave me grace enough to hold
The syrup of energy my muscles floated in.
Though I might tingle with the smell of grass,
Her patience filled my ears with catechism.

The Man of Great Protrusion Recalls the Place
of his Growing Pains and Process

It is still there, beyond the city limits
Of age and Sunday laws, the place
I primed my teen-age paunch
With ten-cent and illegal draughts.

The flies still dip and do and dance
Above the mucous Michie barrels.
Whiskey labels blaze in heraldry,
And plaster chips in flower patterns
Through the bottom of a heavy stein.
Vacation summers we would thump in
Like great Gila monsters from our jobs,
And let the steam rise through our ribs.

I have grown beyond this place
In both capacity and measurement,
But somewhere, tucked in deep,
That first soft spot is down beneath it all.

The Drunkard to his Gelded Cat

Scat! You stinking prune-nutted cadger. Scat!
Go claw some unsuspecting rodent
For your meal, you dud, you nuck, you cat!
I am too fried to even stew a linnet.

Go swish your tail into a wall plug,
Mendicant mumper, solicitous scab!
Go tell your sad tale to the rug,
Petitional pothunter, supplicant tab!

You cannot charm me from this chair,
You impotent, testicless tom,
So hide in your secret ball of hair,
For tomorrow the hangover comes!

Poem for Hartville, Ohio

Praise land. Beard-black and fine,
It yields and yields to the Amish,
While pool halls wither in the town.
Hartville is straight with the presence
Of Fellows. They seem thrusted
Into furrows complete with hoe and hat.
They pray the shoots from seed husks
In the green upon green within green
Of Ohio, in Springtime, which is
Very, very green. Watch for them,
Their buggies rutting the softest shoulders.
Wait for them on hills, at crossings.
Remember you, not they are in the way
In Hartville, in Springtime, in Ohio.

Put God aside and think what makes
The aspen shake. Fear of God, you say?
Oh hell, a breeze from the pagan sea!

Put Him aside again and think what makes
The eagle rise. Faith in God, you say?
Oh damn, a whorish sparrow in the sky!

Put Him aside once more and think what makes
The flowers bloom. The hand of God, you say?
Oh fiends, the lust of spring I say!

Put Him aside a last time and think what makes
The fire in hell. The wrath of God, you say?
Oh praise, you have converted me!

IV

THE POET PROJECTED INTO SHAPES

Keats in Rome

No rusty folio nor fleck of rose
Upon a linen frock. Keats bleeds!
His life is spattered in his kerchief.
A thousand miles from Wentworth Place
He coughs in the Italian morning.
The sun through his eyelids is Fanny,
The flap of the birds on the Pincian,
The dregs in his cup of tea are Fanny,
The heat of his brow as much Fanny
As sickness.
              Who could kiss in letters
Or love with words? Keats dies trying.

In Rome the couples wash their faces
At the fountains and kiss in the November sun.
In Rome the moon draws lovers
To the shadows under balconies,
While Keats dies hard above them.

Blues for Charlie Christian

Charlie rubbed his hands across the sky of Oklahoma,
And let it curve his itchy fingernails.
He sprang the blues loose in Dakota
To coil out through the grinning scales.

Let it quiver like a snake, he thought,
Let the poison drown me. I'll throw
Out what was in me the first day
I rapped a chord. Oil a dream, old Joe!

Charlie's here with blues from Bismark
And the Okie cities. There's no silky twisting
Here where flats go grinding dust.
Oil a dream, Joe. Charlie's got the misting

Blues, and time is stacking up.
He'll hand you more than swinging fists if
You let him moan alone. Go whistle down
The limited when Charlie blows a city riff.

In the midnight of the buildings he tumbled
Down his strings, and rattled songs toward
Memphis and the Apple, and they saw he struck
Out diamonds with his fingertips of chord.

Go down, Joe, he thought, and push
The notes together. Time's coming and makes
Your Charlie breathe his blood. Got no time
To jingle ice cubes with the lushy fakes,

Don't even care if Minton clangs
His register in B. There's more to say
Than if I'd live to say it. Because I fade
I'll give them thoughts to play.

Band in Boston, Lord, and Charlie's full
Of bloody air! Oil her, Joe! One more coat
For that tight-strung dream. You know
Charlie's got to end it on the bluest note.

Wordsworth in Summer

"Intensely hot. I made pies in the morning. William went into the wood, and altered his poems."

The Journal of Dorothy Wordsworth,
July 28, 1800

William's lines were simmered like blueberries
That July. Beneath the trees
He smelled the lacquer of their juice,
And heard their seeds fall loose
To crackle like old meters in the heat;
And later on he ate them with his tea.

Juan Belmonte in the Moonlight

In Memoriam
(1892–1962)

Under the cape of the moon he fought them.
Hey toro!
Their horns as black as twelve o'clock,
And their sweat upon his urchin sleeves.
He pressed their snouts against his coat
And curled them round his crooked body
To see the red dwarf stars
Within their eyes. Hey toro!
The dance of youth for the anger
Of beasts, the movement of death
For the thrust of their heads,
The water of night for the coals
In their eyes, the folds of his coat
For the points of their horns. Hey toro!
In Sevilla and Madrid he would
Prick their white hot hearts
To make the crowd go roaring
Like a conch. Hey toro!
But as el matador de luna,
The white assassin with his wooden sword,
In the deep of the night he grew
To greatness—the hero of the dark corrals.

Father Mendel at Brünn

Three to one inside these walls,
The sons of stilted and the long,
One tall, one short to make the talls,
Then three to one the tall ones strong.

What prince of pollen cuts these rules
And overlaps the choice of wind?
Who rubs against the grafting tools
And makes the lighter things rescind?

Three to one outside these walls
And old von Metternich is done.
Now the house of Hapsburg falls
And threes have made the Empire one.

Lord, give me touch to understand,
And I will shed my pruning glove
To feel your ever choosing hand
Count out the strong seed's love.

Three to one inside these walls,
The sons of stilted and the long,
One tall, one short to make the talls,
Then three to one the tall ones strong.

Mr. Handel's Music for the Royal Fireworks

Though gout was twisting at my old age,
Sixteen yards of Green Park wall were moved
To let my public in. And though opacities
Were folding in my eyes, I brought all London
Down to hear my Bourrée and my Minuets.
Then between La Paix and Réjouissance
Old Servandoni touched his punk against the fuse
And pushed the night back up into the sky.

Gog's heart! Never have I seen such
Fuming, cracking, pouring, as if the sun
Had fired a rain of oil. It bent
My quarter notes like wire and hammered
My arpeggi until they came out straighter
Than tenuto notes. We played on
Though Roman candles spit as if the war
Had come again, but when the Temple of the Peace
Began to burn as though it were the paper
Of the treaty, then the music stopped abruptio.

Down Piccadilly, Pall Mall, and St. James we ran
Like infantry before a Prussian volley.
And I, my new wig burning with my suite,
And my old joints grinding with each stride,
Recalled the day I played my music on the water,
And deemed it far safer than fire.

Johnny Blood

Johnny Blood,
That bow-legged, demon halfback
By way of Gary, Pottsville and Duluth,
Made our women, drank our gin
And hacked our line to pieces.

All this and he was long gone
Monday morning, with a head fake
And a stiff arm, leaving panties,
Empty jugs, and broken tackles
In his tracks.

            Four touchdowns,
And four women starry-eyed;
Four empty rotgut bottles and
Four quarters of his pumping knees
Gave us our taste and fill of
Johnny Blood.

First Mate Joseph Conrad

My legs are worn to dangling ropes
By this ball bearing sea which rolls
The world against the frictional sky.
Even these waves which mime
The quarters of the moon are not enough
To hook it to a stop.
                              All is curves and angles.
Even our unwrenchable wake would lead us
To believe our course was like the flicking
Of the sharks and salmons—the creatures
Of this watery, violent world, who know
The tints and foul moods of the sea.

But more than this sea is mutable.
I have stood upon the bridge and watched
The subtle, cloudless sky grow dark
And crack like rarest china, and until
The storm had snuffed my smoking pipe
I did not realize the change.

There are no straight lines in the sky,
Or in the sea, or in these seamen.
All is by degrees, so changeable
The senses are like earth worms
Nosed against a boulder.

I have been too long upon the water.
Death and danger ring like children's threats.
Is it presumptuous to think I can do more?
Perhaps some day I'll catch the corner
Of the sky and sea before it moves
Beyond my reach.

Buckskin Man

He made his cut so lean through trees
A cold knife could not fit through it again.
He carried Osage mud to the hissing of the Snake,
And locked his path behind him all the way.
Whiskey fumes were folded with his campfire,
But he never let smoke dangle to the east.
The iris of a Pawnee was a shade above
A squirrel eye, but slick as any Downy
With a maple knot, he'd take them both
Out with a flicker of his cap and ball.
On summer nights the stars would suckle
At his eyes, but one night in the early
Forties he wrung two hairy pawpaws
Out of earth to see a blazer stretch
Itself through half the sizzling sky.
He thought he'd rather look down
On a field full of Apache braves,
Than look up to feel a rabid star
Tear him from the suck of earth.
He wandered on a string of green
Where each eyeflick tied a new knot,
Where lightning laced the thunder
Of the buffalo as well as clouds.
But people in the east had heard
The green cells turn their telophase,
And someone heard him whistling
From the pockets of his kingdom,
So that soon he heard them spring the leaves
He'd locked so carefully behind him.

Reverend Animus Closes the First Church
of Christ and His Saints

The pews that smelled like melting Brie,
Like sopped cats in radiator wintertime,
Were never full. Even on Christmas
One could always hear the candles snapping
Through the Glorias, and feel the treble sneezes
Of the organist. My congregation passioned with
Ladies who had either lost or lost control
Of their stogey-scented husbands. Vociferous
In sanctity, they could not fill my nave.

It grieves me more for me than God
To close these heavy doors. He knows
My hymn books were well-thumbed
And my sermons full of rhetoric and reason.
That was my energy and heart, not His.

The ladies will go on in vocal holiness,
God will smile in His infinitude,
But my sermons will bounce in numbness
From the unseen stars. That part of me
Is gone forever. Years ago, in deep theology,
I laid the pious plans which somehow failed.
I would have had them love God with their fear.
I would have had God look like me to them.

Notes Toward a Biography of Christiaan Radius, Near-Sighted Astronomer

Radius, Christiaan Ole (rá' dĕ̄ ŏŏs). 1528–1594.
Born to Jorgen and Karen in the hamlet
Of Helsingor, where midwives pruned him
By bloody light of the sword-tailed comet
Which had induced his mother's labor.

Apprenticed to a Slesvig glazier,
He learned to grind his lenses
On the bottom of his master's bottles.
Then, in his nineteenth year,
He took an ax up to his attic room
And chopped his future through the roof.

He counted a hundred stars
With his home made alidades,
And swore he'd charted heaven
From God's throne out to its gates.
He called an eclipse fifty times,
But the troll sun disobeyed him,
Being but a tunnel plumb to hell,
Or so he said.

One could say he spent his lifetime
Proving that the world was triangular
In shape, that there were wingèd mice
Upon the moon, that stars were
Shavings from the sun.

One could say that when he died
He had a vision that the comets
Rang like silver gongs in tribute
To his careful scrutiny.

But this biography, no doubt,
Will not be written,
As who would put the flesh
Around this skeleton of facts?
A man is not remembered
For his terrible misjudgements,
No matter how much innocence
He mixes with his ignorance.

Pacini and his Shipmates Tell of the Storm

Pacini

Our staysails cracked like teacups
As the storm came through them
And sailed us on our starboard.
The nudge of whale or reef
Never split a strut like that.
O Dio! The belly of the clouds
Dropped out and we were tucked
Between the water and the water,
Wandering like a one-eyed gull.
We flew upon the blunt waves,
Then fell to take the sharp ones
On our backs like Saracen blades.
The wet wind plucked our clew lines
As the night fell. The sea foam
Buffed the blurry stars. Till dawn
The cold wind clacked the hatches,
And the moon flew backwards through
The clouds like a strong, luminous seabird.

Dominino

Jesu, Maria!
The wind huffed our prayers into Carthago.
It took our Hail Marys word by word
And blew them where the Virgin never
Heard them. God had his deaf ear
Turned toward the sea, and the waves
Were free to hate us.

Vivani

In Ancona once I saw an unwed mother
Tossed and beaten by a crowd;
But what had been our ship's sin,
Save she rode the water proudly?

Pacini

At dawn the cold sea sheathed its waves,
Running blue again. The wind drew in
Its tongue and pushed the storm beyond
The ship. The gate of rains flew back,
And we passed it like a wall to see
That sun, though two times round
The world, still waited for us
At the other end.

V

THE RIBS OF DEATH

Death-locked crabs flew three ways
When he thudded to the sand
   the first time;
And when he fell again
The seagulls felt a quiver
   in their tongues.
The third time, sick of blades,
And clubs, and knuckles,
He layed down as softly
   as a Poorwill hen,
And all the bones and rattles
In the world could not raise him.
His great black eyes contracted
   to a pinpoint,
And neither clouds, nor sand,
Nor sea could prick them.
When the tide was thin enough
   to see through,
It took his great red bulk to sea.
Behind him rolled the corpses
   of his killers,
They who could not stand
His fingertips as big as knees,
His teeth as big as breast bones,
Nor his heart much larger
   than their heads.

The Invalid in the Garden

Branches crook like blackened digits
At the clouds, and tulips knuckle
In the ground this fall . . .
As last fall . . .
         and all falls.
Apples, acid with the summer,
Pop like sick cicadas.
                I feel death
Like one feels snow when it
Is still high in the mountains.

     Little consolation that
I will not see the tucked eggs
Hatch next spring,
            nor feel
The spray of sun-excited trees,
Nor hear the junco crick
Above his mate.

I could not fold my eggs in bark,
Nor store my life in frozen chambers
For a winter.

When I die this garden dies.

Through this Glass

There is quick beauty in the snapping of a wave tip.
Not even beaks that carve the froth for minnows
Are swift enough to see it, raking bubbles
More for flesh than sea roll. Undone the wave grows

To crack its head so brittle at the birds,
To lock the air, defying one moment in its curl
Before it flattens back to time. And what stars
Could be seen through this glass! What a whirl

Of glossy rainbows to bleed again to grey!
Cold now in air or deep beneath the light,
Water waits an eon for such use; a thousand years
Or more to ride again and be so bright.

The Man in the First Wave

That is no ping of water in a pan.
Lying in the hills are men with eyes
As deep as fluorite, who can see
The surf jump at their squeezings.

What use for me, to turn within the humor
Of their eyes, and curl up like a worm
Within their pupils! The slap of sea
Hammering a fish would mean as much,

The cold cells puckering around the wound.
But from some pulsing socket in the hills,
And twisting through the ragged palms will come
A bullet for the draining of my veins.

What use! My father ran upon a bowstring
And fell before the squinting of an eye,
And he gave the earth no mineral
It did not have before he died.

The Murderous Gardener Shows his Wares
with Pride

Come sir,
See my garden and be free of time.
Age is but increased awareness
Of one's limitations anyhow.

Come see the upas
And the gentle camass
Sifting wind like laurel,
Innocent as sorrel.

See the blackness of the belladonna berries,
Darker than deep wells and moonless nights,
And the purple of the foxglove blossoms,
Sadder than autumn or twilight.

Now, come and rest with me.
We will have some henbane tea,
And a slice of mescal cake
Topped with preserves of sumac.

Sir, do not dull my pleasure
With your gentle company
By saying that my garden fades,
And do not ask for antidotes!
I slaved to make this garden live,
Now you complain because you die!

Apple Blight

Blighted apples will not shine.
Though they are buffed by winds
As diligent as Caesar's valets,
The fog has settled in their skins.

Branches bow down low to death,
Dragged by blighted apples.
Cold leaves curl about the wind,
Strangled by dull apples.

Though apples host the cruelest worms,
The hardest beetles, still they shine,
But when the sickness sweeps the tree
They will not shine, they will not shine.

The Hand on the Tiller

Supposing at midnight the chambers
Of our coxswain's heart spit air
Into his arteries. Then would
The whim of rudder be guided
By the Father, Son, and Holy Ghost?
Then which one would choose rocks,
And which one scissors,
And which one paper?

But hell, that shellback's heart
Is stouter than a rigger's angry fist,
And the fizzling of the falling stars
Across that harp of a moon
Will pluck upon his veins
And keep him lean. Sail on.
To bed, and let that jacky,
Or the Trinity, roll whatever stars
They will above our heads,
And pass whatever squawking ice
Or twittering jungle they will
Across our port holes.

Night Flight of the Consumptive

Sick-a-bed, I hear the cabman's horse
Roll up his foamy lips for apples.
Cats circle, threaten, and attack
Like sirens underneath my window.
The laughter of the whores is steel on steel.
The songs of drunkards are like fingernails
On slate. I live in horror of the hour
Upon the hour when church clocks bark
Dogmatic time with bells and clappers.
I would slant above all cat threats,
Crickets, whore sounds, drunk songs,
Cab rattles, can clatters, and dog murmurs;
Rising past the lovers' steamy windows,
Beyond the roof tiles, through the clouds,
And past the moon to the maw
Of forever behind the stars,
Where lungs are clear of fire and fluid,
And life is to sleep and sleep.

The Splitting of the Pirate Gillian

The meat of Gillian is gull dung now.
His bones are the light of the moon.

Squaring the sun with his silver buckle,
He dared to rise against giants,
And fell in halves to the east and west.

Now his ragged innards float like giblets
On the sea, and his sinews are unstrung
From his great galleon.